How to Choose a Bible

Woodrow Kroll

BACK TO THE BIBLE
LINCOLN, NE 68501

17,000 printed to date—1995
(1150-224—4M—55)
ISBN 0-8474-0891-4

Printed in the United States of America.

Introduction

What's the most important purchase you will make in life? If you own your home, you'll likely say that was your most important purchase. After all, it costs the most. If you don't own a house but do own a car, you may think that is the most important purchase you can make. But if you are a Christian, the most important purchase is your Bible.

A Bible does not cost as much as a house or a car, but houses and cars cannot tell you how to get to heaven or give you insight in how to have abundant life in Christ before you get there. No, your Bible may not be the most expensive purchase, but it is the most important.

While everyone who owns a house or car shops around and gets as much information about their purchase before they make it, most people don't do much research before they buy a Bible. So they don't know which Bible is best for them.

That is why this book examines how to choose a Bible that is best for you. My intent is to help you understand what is available so that you may choose the kind of Bible that will best facilitate your personal study of God's Word.

Chapter 1

Choosing a Version

Today, most of the world has a wide variety of choices when selecting a Bible. There are dozens of versions available. Let's look at how some of them came to be, and then we'll see which is best for you. Of the more popular versions today, here are some of the ones you are most likely to be interested in when choosing a Bible.

The King James Version

The most universally accepted English translation of all time, the King James Version (KJV) is also known as the Authorized Version. This edition of the Bible was commissioned by James I, King of Great Britain, France and Ireland, in the 1600s. Fifty-four translators used the Old Testament Masoretic Text and the New Testament Textus Receptus to complete this translation in 1611.

Born in the "age of literature," at the dawn of the Enlightenment, the KJV is often described as reverent, majestic and poetic. This was the era of Shakespeare; language flourished to the most eloquent level in history. It is also for that reason that some people today find the KJV more difficult to read. When a reading comprehension scale was devised, the KJV was judged to be at a 12th-grade level, whereas many adults read at an 8th-grade level or lower.

If you are like me, you grew up reading the King James Bible and memorized many verses from it. I still enjoy reading it, but a number of good translations have been released recently.

The New International Version

Published in 1978, the New International Version, popularly known as the NIV, was commissioned by the International Bible Society. They looked to 115 conservative, evangelical scholars for the translation work, using the Masoretic Text and the New Testament published by the United Bible Societies.

The NIV has now edged out the KJV as the most frequently purchased Bible in North America. It is written in comfortable language and therefore is easy to read and understand, with a seventh-grade reading level. This is its most appreciated feature.

The New King James Version

A version rapidly becoming more popular is the New King James, known as the NKJV. Thomas Nelson Publishers commissioned a team of 130 scholars to prepare an updated version of the KJV, and it was released in 1982. The NKJV is easier to read (eighth-grade level) than the KJV but still retains some of the elegant, literary style of its distinguished predecessor.

The NKJV is based on the Masoretic Text for the Old Testament and the Textus Receptus for the New Testament, with alternative readings from the majority Greek texts. This version is appreciated by those who love the King James but are not looking for Shakespearean language.

The New American Standard Version

When the Lockman Foundation sponsored and released the New American Standard Bible (NASB) in 1971, it was thought that this would challenge the King James in popularity. And while the NASB is widely used, it ranks behind the KJV, NIV and NKJV in sales.

This translation is easier to read than the 1901 American Standard Version but is still at an 11th-grade level. Fifty-four conservative and evangelical scholars used the Old Testament Masoretic Text and the 23rd edition of the Nestle Greek New Testament in translating the NASB.

One of the key features of this version is that it translates the Hebrew, Aramaic and Greek wording of ancient texts as accurately and as literally as possible into English. Therefore, it is well suited for in-depth Bible study.

There are many other versions that could be mentioned: The New Revised Standard Version, Today's English Version, The Amplified Version, the New Century Version and the Living Bible, for example. However, which version you choose may depend on which you most trust—and that leads to another discussion.

So many manuscripts

I have mentioned the Old Testament Masoretic Text, the Textus Receptus and the Nestle Greek Text.

What are all these manuscripts, and why are they important? This is the crux of the version controversy.

The fundamental difference between the NIV, New English Bible, NASB and the KJV is that they are based on different forms of the Greek text. These are sometimes called families of texts.

The King James is closely associated with the Textus Receptus, which is Latin for "received text," the text received by most people of that time. Actually, the Textus Receptus was not published until 13 years after the first edition of the KJV. It represents the traditional text.

In 1853 a young scholar named Fenton John Anthony Hort teamed with an older scholar, Brooke Foss Westcott, and proposed the theory that certain manuscripts were of greater accuracy and therefore of greater weight than the majority of manuscripts. Known as the Westcott-Hort theory, this approach to selecting specific manuscripts has been the basis for the later versions of the Bible.

With more than 5,000 Greek manuscripts of the New Testament to study, Westcott and Hort believed the manuscripts that followed Alexandrian and Western patterns were better than those that followed the Syrian or Traditional patterns. So, for instance, the NIV was translated predominantly from a different group of manuscripts than the KJV was.

Which family of manuscripts is best? Contrary to all the controversy and numerous tracts, booklets and books written to justify one family of manuscripts and vilify the other, the bottom line is we do not know. They are all copies of the original writings, or autographs, of Scripture.

Since no one has the autographs, we are left to study copies of those manuscripts. While strong arguments are made on each side of this controversy, any honest person must admit that all of our arguments are secondary. Without the original writings, we are simply expressing faith in the case for one set of copies over another.

It may surprise you that there are about 200,000 variant readings in the manuscripts of the New Testament. These variant readings are both between these families of manuscripts and within them. That may shock you, but that is not as bad as it seems. For example, if a single word is misspelled in the same way in 3,000 separate manuscripts, it is counted as 3,000 variant readings, when actually it is only one.

The upside and downside

Obviously, there are benefits to the variety of versions from which you may choose, and there is a downside as well. The upside is that you can choose a Bible that you understand and know that it is the true Word of God. You can compare versions and get a better understanding of a verse even if you don't read Greek or Hebrew. In your private study of the Bible, you can contrast how different versions translate the same passage.

There is a downside, however. When everyone used the King James Version, it was easy for the leader of a Bible study group to point out a word and have everyone focus on it. Today, that word may have three or four variations in the same study group because three or four versions are present. Also, it's almost impossible now for a congregation to read

God's Word in unison in a church service. There is a cacophony of sounds when everyone is reading out of different versions.

Whichever version you choose, remember that there is a huge difference between owning a Bible and reading it. Select a version based on your beliefs, and then be faithful to read and memorize God's Word. After all, God doesn't call us to add to or settle the version controversy; He does call us to let His Word be a lamp to our feet and a light to our path (Ps. 119:105). Let your Bible be your light.

Chapter 2

Choosing the Right Features

Once you settle on a particular version, you are still faced with some big decisions. What features do you want in your Bible? You may be surprised at how diverse Bibles have become in the last decade or so. There are many more features than there are versions.

For example, will you choose a wide-margin Bible, a slimline Bible, a pocket Bible or a giant-print Bible? What about the cover? Do you want bonded leather, genuine cowhide or Kivar calfskin? These variations allow you to select just the right Bible for you; but since there are so many options, it is helpful to be aware of all the options before you choose your Bible.

Bible publishers

You may be surprised to know that, just like the number of Bible versions, there are dozens of Bible publishers. Some of these companies do nothing but publish Bibles. Here are some of the major names in Bible publishing today: Cambridge, Oxford, Riverside, Tyndale, Holman, Word, Kirkbride, World, Moody, Zondervan and Nelson. And these are just the major publishers. Other groups, including Bible societies, also publish the Bible.

Bible size

An important consideration is the size of Bible you choose. How big should it be? That depends on how you plan to use it.

The conventional size for a Bible is 6 x 9 inches, but I have both larger and smaller Bibles. One of my favorites is the Nelson Slimline Reference Bible. It measures only 5 1/4 x 7 7/8 x 5/8 inches. It's the perfect size when you don't need a large Bible.

You can get pocket Bibles that fit in a coat pocket or purse. World Bible Publishers advertises the world's smallest pocket Bible, the size of an audio cassette but 5/8-inch thick. World also publishes the Ultra-Trim Bible, just 3 3/8 x 7 x 1/2 inches, perfect for the inside pocket of a man's suit.

Type size

The older I get the more important type size becomes. Perhaps you have experienced this too. I have good news for you. There are plenty of Bibles available for people who have stretched their arms as far as they can, donned a pair of magnifying glasses and still have trouble reading the Bible.

Most Bibles have an average type size of 8 or 9 points. That is readable for most people, but if you are having trouble with print that small, almost every Bible publisher has a giant-print edition of each version they publish. The giant-print is usually 14-point type, but I have one that is 18 point. It's just right for preaching. I never have trouble seeing my Bible.

Cover and binding

As important as page size and type size are, equally important in selecting a Bible is the cover and binding. Choosing the right cover and binding can double the life of your Bible.

Perhaps you aren't as hard on a Bible as I am. My Bible travels with me in carry-on luggage and on the front seat of my car and is handled daily in devotion and study. I need a solid binding and a durable cover.

Here are some of the cover and binding options available to you.

Genuine leather — select, first-quality animal hides known for strength and grained texture.

Bonded leather — a high-quality, extremely durable material made from leather fibers bonded with adhesive and pressed into flat sheets.

Berkshire leather — a supple pigskin with a smooth, even grain.

Imitation leather — a coated, man-made material that resembles real leather and is durable and easily cleaned.

Calfskin — sometimes called "water buffalo calf-skin," this is my favorite. It is one of the most handsome and durable binding leathers used for Bibles. It looks exquisite in colors due to its subtle two-toned effect and wide arrays of grains.

French Morocco — a high-quality sheepskin (also called "skiver"), it is butter soft, naturally flexible and quite durable. It is usually found on more expensive editions of the Bible.

Kivar — an acrylic, impregnated latex base material that is rugged and used on softcover Bibles.

Hardcover — a less-expensive cover made of in-flexible binder's boards covered with cloth or imitation leather.

The more you use your Bible, the better the cover and binding you should choose. The pages of your

Bible will last much longer than the cover and binding will, so choose well.

Bible features

There are also many study-help features you may select when choosing a Bible. Think through what you need most and select a Bible with only those features you need. Here are some of the more popular features.

Bible dictionary — an alphabetical listing of characters, places and terminology that help you understand general and background information about the Bible.

Concordance — an alphabetical word list used to locate a verse. A concordance lists the places in the text where significant words are found. This can be an indispensable tool for Bible study.

Thumb index — an index to help the reader quickly find his place, similar to the index used in some dictionaries.

Presentation page — a decorated page for inscribing the names of the giver and recipient and the date of the gift. This is helpful if you are giving a Bible as a gift to someone else.

Pronouncing Bible — any Bible that marks the vowel sounds and stressed syllables, as in a dictionary. This can be useful for correctly pronouncing all the names in the genealogies, for example.

Red-letter edition — a Bible in which the words of Christ are printed in red, while the rest of the text is printed in black.

Reference Bible — a Bible that includes references, usually in a center column, to guide the reader to other Scripture passages where similar subjects are treated.

Wide margin — a Bible with an inch or more of white space around three sides of the text where you can write notes. I use this Bible frequently in preaching, writing my sermon notes adjacent to the text.

Bible land maps — a series of maps placed in the back of the Bible to provide the reader with a ready geographical reference to the Ancient Near East, Palestine, the journeys of Paul and more.

Which features you select will depend on how you use your Bible. For example, if you have a complete concordance and are using your Bible for personal study at home, you will likely not use the Bible concordance. But such a concordance is helpful while you are away from home. Bible land maps are always helpful, and I recommend them for every Bible. Also helpful are the references placed near the text to similar subjects.

A thumb index, on the other hand, is not helpful for me because the indentation reduces the amount of margin space in which I can write notes.

There is much more to be said about what to look for in a Bible, such as gilt or silver edges, button flaps or zippers, colored covers, etc. You can personalize your Bible in many ways. Before you buy a Bible, decide which features you want, and then purchase a Bible with just those features.

Then read your Bible every day, taking advantage of those features. It won't matter what you have in your Bible if you don't read it.

Chapter 3

Choosing the Right
Study Bible

Few Bibles come with just the Word of God printed in them. Most have study notes, references, charts, graphs and illustrations to help you better understand Scripture. Since so much is available, you may have trouble deciding whether or not you should buy a study Bible. And if you decide it would be helpful to you, which one should you buy?

These are good questions, and I pray that this survey of reference and study Bibles today will help clear the air for you. I want you to make an informed choice when you purchase a Bible. After all, it's the most important purchase of your Christian life.

Here are some specialty Bibles you may be aware of. They aren't for everyone, but one of them may be for you.

Devotional Bibles

The Family Devotions Bible was developed for parents who want to teach their children godly values through biblically based devotions. It was the first family devotional to combine the complete Bible text with devotional stories. It features 365 family devotions alongside the Living Bible text and is fantastic for teaching families godly values. *The Family Devotions Bible* is published by Tyndale.

The One-Year Bible, also published by Tyndale, is the current best-selling devotional Bible. It's easy to read, and each daily reading includes a portion from the Old Testament, New Testament, Psalms and Proverbs. It's a great way to become acquainted with the entire Bible and will help you read through the Bible in a year.

The Women's Devotional Bible, published by Zondervan, is advertised as a devotional Bible for, by and about today's Christian woman. It features devotional meditations written by more than 100 well-known Christian women. The devotional meditations for each weekday are located near the designated Scripture reading. Plus there is a "Weekending" feature—a devotional meditation for each weekend—providing an entire year of devotional readings.

The Encounter Bible is published by Holman and is on the "through-the-Bible-in-a-year" plan with devotions for a lifetime. Designed especially for young people, it teaches how to have a quiet time, focuses on specific passages for memory verses and has a devotional subject index. Your teenager will benefit from it greatly.

Speciality Bibles

In addition to devotional Bibles, there are other Bibles published for a specific audience. If you fall into any of the specialty categories, you may find one of the following Bibles helpful to you.

The Student Bible was designed by Zondervan to overcome the obstacles to regular Bible reading that young people mention most frequently. In addition to its overview of all the books of the Bible and a guide to Jesus' ministry, this Bible uses a unique Three-Track system for reading the Bible. It's great for getting young students into Bible study.

The Comparative Study Bible is also published by Zondervan. It features the complete texts of the New International, New American Standard, Amplified and King James versions in parallel columns on facing pages. This enables you to compare versions when you want to discover the various ways a particular word is translated.

The KJV Christian Worker's New Testament is the constant companion of anyone who wants to share the plan of salvation with others. It uses an instant reference system that marks the subject matter of a verse and links it to the next verse about that subject. This enables you to move from one point in the plan of salvation to another without difficulty. It's a wonderful evangelistic tool.

Akin to this is *The NIV Counselor's New Testament*. This Bible is used by pastors and laypeople who advise others. It uses a chain-reference system to guide you to the 99 most helpful topics referred to by biblical counselors. Each passage on the key topic is color-highlighted in the text. You'll appreciate this handy help when counseling others about a variety of subjects, such as doubt or depression.

One of my favorite speciality Bibles is *The Christian Life Bible*, published by Thomas Nelson. Its prominent feature is the "Master Outlines and Study Notes," written by Porter Barrington. In these 52 easy-to-understand outlines, Dr. Barrington identifies and explains the cornerstone theological truths of Christianity.

They are arranged so you can proceed step by step through your study, building a solid foundation for your Christian life. Dr. Barrington gave my wife and me a copy of this Bible shortly after it was released in 1985, and we have used it profitably ever since.

Study Bibles

The last category of Bibles you should be familiar with before you choose one is study Bibles. I will mention only four such Bibles, although there are many others. You can rely on any of these to aid in your study of the Scriptures.

The Open Bible is a treasure trove of useful information about the Bible. Published by Thomas Nelson, this study Bible contains a 300-page topical index, a Visual Survey of the Bible, the Christian's Guide to the New Life and other maps, charts and word studies—right at your fingertips. For a sweeping overview of the Scriptures that pinpoints the answers you seek, you can't beat *The Open Bible*. I have one and use it often.

Zondervan sent me *The Life Application Bible* soon after it was released, and it instantly became a favorite. It features an overview, vital statistics, a blueprint (outline), megathemes and a map for each book of the Bible. This alone makes it a valuable reference tool, but there's more. Application and explanatory study notes, profiles of biblical characters, a harmony of the Gospels incorporated at sectional headings in the Gospels and charts and diagrams throughout make this a Bible everyone can benefit from.

Akin to that is *The Word in Life Study Bible*. When it was released by Thomas Nelson, I received a copy to examine and found it to be equally helpful. Its purpose is to help you discover ways to relate the Word of God to you and the world you live in. *The Word in Life Study Bible* helps you get a clear understanding of the Scriptures by focusing on those things surrounding the biblical narrative. For example, features about the people, places and customs of Jesus' day teach about life in the first century. You'll discover that people 2,000 years ago weren't much different than we are today.

The Ryrie Study Bible, published by Moody Press, is perhaps the most popular study Bible today. It has been a best-seller for many years. This practical study Bible is available in the four most popular translations and contains a library of information invaluable to your understanding of the Bible. It is the one theologian's study Bible a non-theologian can understand. The outlines and introductions will prepare you to explore each book of the Bible, and thousands of insightful notes explain difficult passages.

We need to thank God for the effort and time expended by the authors and publishers alike to bring us so many useful tools for Bible study. But just like any tool, they will do you no good if you don't use them. So choose a Bible that meets your needs, and then meet those needs every day.

Chapter 4

Breaking in a New Bible

We have come in our study of choosing a Bible to a final, important consideration. After you choose the version, the specific features and the type of study Bible you want, after you purchase your Bible and set it before you, you'll discover the joy of opening a new Bible for the first time.

I love the smell of a new Bible, don't you? Especially if it has a leather cover. My heart is always quickened when I smell the delightful aroma of new leather and India paper.

Opening your new Bible without damaging it can be tricky. So here are some tips on breaking in a new Bible.

Gilded edges stick together

If your Bible has gold or silver edges on the pages, some of those pages will probably stick together. That is because of the process used to gild the pages. But if you separate them too quickly, you may tear the corners of each page. That will leave you with too much page on one side and too little on the other. Here's what to do.

When you find pages stuck together at the gilded edge, gently use the cutting edge of a sharp knife to separate the pages at the edge of the paper. This should free your pages without damage.

For me, getting a new Bible is like getting a new car. When I buy a car, even if it's new only to me, I dread putting that first scratch or dent on it. After the first dent, I'm not as careful or concerned about the others. Likewise, pages of your Bible will eventually get rumpled or torn, but you don't want that to happen soon after you have opened it for the first time.

Bindings break easily

The easiest way to ruin a new Bible is to break its binding. Eventually this will lead to a loss of pages.

One of my favorite Bibles was a red Scofield Reference Bible I received when I was a teenager. I loved that King James Bible. I have ink smudges, erasure marks, notes, poems and quotes written over every available inch. It was the first real study Bible I had after I was old enough to begin digging in the Word for myself. Unfortunately, the binding broke on the Bible, and today the Book of Genesis and half of Exodus is missing.

To avoid a similar fate, take great care in opening your Bible for the first time. It's important you break in a Bible the right way, and here's how.

After you have made sure that no pages are sticking together because of the gilded edges, place your Bible with the spine on a table. Move the back cover to the right and the front cover to the left while holding the pages of your Bible in a vertical position.

Don't push the covers all the way to the table. That will break the binding. In time, they will be able to touch the table simultaneously.

Next, take a few pages in the back of your Bible in your fingers and press them toward the back cover. Repeat the process with a few pages in the front, pressing them toward the front cover. Do this with a few more pages, back then front, back then front. Eventually you will press all the pages toward the cover until you end up somewhere near the first chapter of Isaiah with no more pages to press. This is a gentle way to break in a new Bible without breaking the binding.

Bible pages absorb well

Have you noticed that many of your old Bibles are smudged or stained with grease? Perhaps the ink from your notes has bled on the paper. That is because most pages of a Bible are absorbent. How can you avoid this problem with a new Bible? Here are some tips.

One way to avoid the "bleeding ballpoint" is to use a pencil. It won't be as visible or permanent as a pen, but it won't bleed either. Perhaps you will choose to use colored pencils to indicate different kinds of markings. I've done that with good results.

Here's something else you can do. In several of my Bibles, I've used India ink, which will not bleed through the page. It's a solid, black pigment used in drawing and lettering. However, India ink can be messy, especially if you must use a quill and inkwell. I have drawings in some of my older Bibles I can't quite identify. I've finally decided they are ink blots!

The best way to avoid such blots is to use a special pen with drawing ink. A German company named Staedtler makes a pen called "Marsmatic 700" with varying thicknesses of point. Fill the pen with Staedtler Marsmatic 745 drawing ink and write as if you were writing with a ballpoint pen. The ink will not bleed through, it is permanent, and if you vary the size of the point on the pen, you can vary the width of what you write. I use the .80 size for major headings and the smaller .50 size for subheadings.

The tips in this chapter will help your Bible last longer. But don't worry about keeping your Bible spotless. A well-worn copy of God's Word is a sign of a well-worked servant of God.

Conclusion

Frequently, people send me pamphlets and book-lets attacking one version or another. Every argument for which version is the right one or the best one rests on faith. It's apparent that many Christians read one book or one pamphlet that supports their position, and they use what the author said as a point of attack on other versions. It's also obvious they never read a book that presents the evidence for the position oppo-site to theirs.

Allow me to suggest two books to you. Wilbur Pickering's *The Identity of the New Testament Text*, pub-lished by Thomas Nelson, is a reasoned defense of the validity of the King James Version. If you have not read it, you should. An equally important book is D. A. Carson's *The King James Version Debate: A Plea for Realism*, published by Baker. These two books will give you facts without sensationalism.

Choose a version of the Bible that you feel comfort-able with, regardless of what others say. Choose the features of the Bible that meet your needs. And choose the study references of a Bible that will help you get the most out of your Bible.

But whatever you do, use the Bible you choose. Dust on the Bible reflects dust in the heart. Don't just buy a Bible; know it in your head, stow it in your heart, show it in your life, and sow it in the world.

Back to the Bible is a nonprofit ministry dedicated to Bible teaching, evangelism and edification of Christians worldwide.

If we may assist you in knowing more about Christ and the Christian life, please write to us without obligation.

Back to the Bible
P.O. Box 82808
Lincoln, NE 68501